AURA GARDEN HANDBOOKS

Camellias

ALAN TOOGOOD

Editor Maggie Daykin

Designers James Marks, Steve Wilson

Published by Aura Editions
2 Derby Road
Greenford, Middlesex

Produced by Marshall Cavendish Books Limited
58 Old Compton Street
London W1V 5PA
in association with ICI Garden Products

Printed in Italy by Amilcare Pizzi SpA, Milan

Front cover: Camellia japonica 'Tricolor'
Title page: Camellia japonica
Back cover: Camellia x. williamsii 'Donation'

CONTENTS

Introduction   4
Varieties of Camellia   8
Camellias for the Specialist   12
Camellias in the Garden   14
Choosing Quality Plants   16
Growing Camellias   18
Pruning   24
Camellias in Containers   26
After of Container Plants   30
Camellias in the Greenhouse   32
Making More Plants   34
Pests and Diseases   37
Sixty of the Best   38
Index   48

INTRODUCTION

Over the centuries camellias have been in and out of fashion, but today they enjoy great popularity. And small wonder: these evergreen shrubs with handsome, glossy leaves flower at a time when many other plants are resting – during the autumn, winter or spring, depending on variety.

The cup- or bowl-shaped blooms of the camellia take various forms, such as single, where there is only a single row of petals, or double, when the flowers are composed of many rows of petals. The flowers come in shades of pink, red and white, and a few varieties are scented. You may be surprised to learn also that the tea plant is a camellia (correctly known as *C. sinensis*, it is a native of China).

Camellias are easy to grow, but it is essential that they have a lime- or chalk-free soil (in other words, acid conditions). So, if your garden soil is either limy or chalky, do not attempt to grow camellias in beds or borders; instead plant them in pots or tubs of acid compost, for they make ideal container plants (see page 26).

Most camellias are hardy out of doors in Britain, although there are a few tender kinds which need the protection of a greenhouse. Most popular are the varieties of the common camellia (*C. japonica*), which is the hardiest.

However, even the hardy varieties can be flowered under glass if grown in pots or tubs, and are ideal for providing winter or spring colour in a cool conservatory or greenhouse.

Camellias are named after a German missionary and botanist, George Joseph Kamel (1661-1706), who travelled in Asia, and indeed camellias are natives mainly of China, but also of Japan, Korea and India.

ABOVE RIGHT 'Yours Truly', a delightful pink and white, semi-double variety of *Camellia japonica*. A slower grower, it makes an upright bush of ideal size for the small to medium garden.
RIGHT *C. japonica* 'Adolphe Audusson'. An old variety that makes a large bush with arching branches. The semi-double red blooms appear in mid-season.

Camellia sinensis, the tea plant which, for over 4000 years, has been used by the Chinese for making tea. The form grown in this country is a compact, slow growing shrub, the small white flowers appearing in the spring. The size and shape of the leaf varies according to the shrub's geographical location.

In the wild, where many are capable of growing into trees, they grow on rugged hillsides in woods and forests, in shade or partial shade, and in well-drained soil rich in leaf-mould. The areas they inhabit are subject to very high rainfall, high humidity, hot summers and cold winters. These conditions give an indication of how they should be grown in our gardens, but more of this later.

A brief history In China, the leaves of the tea plant (*C. sinensis*) have been used for making tea over a period of at least 4,000 years. The Chinese also grew ornamental camellias as long ago as A.D. 618. But it was not until 1700 that camellias arrived in England, and then only as dried specimens.

However, many camellias (presumably plants) were sent to England from China and Japan between about 1730 and 1850 and these were used for breeding new varieties.

The early camellias in Britain were grown in warm greenhouses, known as stove houses, where temperatures were kept very high. Too high, in fact, so plants generally died. It was thought at the time that camellias needed plenty of warmth.

Eventually, it was found that camellias could be grown out of doors, but even as recently as the 19th Century many people still considered camellias to be warm-greenhouse plants.

Camellias embellished the large ornate conservatories of the 19th Century but at the turn of the century they lost their popularity. There was a revival of interest from the 1930s and a great deal of breeding has been undertaken in this century, especially from the 1950s; not only in Britain, but also in the USA, Australia and New Zealand. This has resulted in hundreds of varieties being available today.

But what of the future? We could be growing yellow, orange, apricot and peach coloured camellias if breeding from the Chinese golden-yellow camellia (*C. chrysantha*) proves successful. Breeders are certainly excited about the possibilities of new colours.

And it is probably safe to say that more and more varieties will be fragrant – a few scented kinds are available now.

VARIETIES OF CAMELLIA

One of the great attractions of camellia flowers is the diversity of shapes or forms. Some resemble roses, others paeonies and anemones. Some have few petals, others many. And the flowers vary in size, too, according to variety. For instance, some varieties have very large blooms up to 12.5cm (5in) across, like the popular 'Donation'; others have miniature flowers, such as 'Ave Maria' with 5cm (2in) diameter blooms.

In many varieties the stamens (the male organs of the flowers) are numerous, prominent and very attractive, often forming a dense cluster in the centre of the flower. In other varieties, the stamens have become miniature petals, which are correctly known as petaloids, these being mixed with normal petals, creating a most attractive bloom.

All of the varieties mentioned below are included in 'Sixty of the best' on pages 38-47.

Single flowers The simplest form of camellia flower is the single. Such flowers have one row (or perhaps circle would be a better description) of petals and there is a large cluster of stamens in the centre. The variety 'J.C. Williams' is one particularly attractive example.

Semi-double flowers These have two, or sometimes more, circles of petals, and again a conspicuous cluster of stamens in the centre of each bloom. A very well-known variety with this type of flower is 'Donation'.

Formal double flowers Very neat and symmetrical, formal doubles have many overlapping petals forming the flower, all perfectly placed, like tiles on a roof. No stamens are visible. A very good example is 'E.G. Waterhouse'.

Paeony forms As their name suggests, the flowers resemble paeonies.

The paeony forms are split into two groups.

Loose paeony: a good example here is the variety 'Drama Girl'. The petals are not tightly overlapping, so the flower is rather loose. There may be a mixture of petals and stamens, perhaps with petaloids as well.

Full paeony: the blooms consist of a mass of petals, petaloids and stamens, or petals and petaloids. The blooms are most attractive, and a good example of a variety with this type of flower is 'Anticipation'.

Anemone form So named because the blooms resemble flowers of certain anemones. A typical variety is 'Elegans'. There may be one or more circles of large petals on the outside of the bloom, while in the centre is a mass of petaloids and stamens.

Rose form double These rose-like blooms consist of a central cluster of stamens surrounded by overlapping petals. The flower is very formal and regular, with perfectly placed petals. A superb variety with this type of flower is 'Joan Trehane'.

ABOVE *Camellia × williamsii* 'Joan Trehane', a vigorous rose form double with pink blooms mid-season.
LEFT *C. japonica* 'Drama Girl' bears very large, salmon-rose pink flowers mid-season. Best grown under glass.
RIGHT *C. japonica* 'C.M. Wilson', which has large, anemone form blooms of pale pink at mid-season. A slow-growing spreader.

The Common Camellia The common camellia (*C. japonica*) is a native of Japan, but is naturalized in China, and bears single red flowers. However, it is the varieties which are grown, and there are hundreds of them.

The most popular of all camellia varieties, they are also the hardiest, and recommended for all sizes of garden. Height and spread are 1.8-3.6m (6-12ft).

They are noted for their handsome glossy foliage, and flower in autumn, winter or spring, according to variety. The varieties are classified as early flowering (that is, autumn flowering), mid-season (the winter period), and late (spring).

Although varieties of the common camellia are easily grown, tough plants, the flowers are soon damaged by hard frosts. It is therefore recommended that in really cold areas, the plants are flowered in a cold greenhouse to protect the blooms. Slight heat could be given in really severe weather.

Choosing varieties can be difficult as there are so many. On pages 40-44 you will find reliable and free-flowering varieties, some old, some new. All are available from specialist camellia growers, and you will also find some of them offered in garden centres. You won't go wrong with any of them.

Williamsii camellias Virtually as popular as varieties of the common camellia, the group known as the *C. x williamsii* hybrids have been created from *C. japonica* and *C. saluenensis*. Hybridizing was begun by Mr J.C. Williams, of Caerhays, Cornwall, round about 1930.

The williamsii camellias are among the hardiest available, and are suited to outdoor growing in all parts of Britain.

The flowering period is autumn to spring, depending on variety, and the spectacular large blooms have the pleasing habit of falling as they fade, so that the bushes are not rendered unsightly by dead blooms. They are extremely free flowering, the glossy foliage being almost hidden at flowering time.

Williamsii camellias can be grown as free-standing shrubs, or against a wall. Height, according to variety, is in the region of 1.8-2.4m (6-8ft), and spread varies from 1.2-1.8m (4-6ft). Good varieties are given on page 45.

Species and their hybrids So far we have been considering the two most popular groups of camellias – the common camellia and the williamsii hybrids. But there are other species that are well worth growing, and some have produced very notable hybrids and varieties.

'Cornish Snow', is a beautiful single camellia, and a hybrid between *C. saluenensis* and *C. cuspidata*. It is early to late flowering, the small white flowers being produced over a very long period. A great attraction, too, is the foliage – the young leaves are flushed with purple. It is of moderate stature, the height and spread being 2.4-3m (8-10ft), and it forms a rounded bush. 'Cornish Snow' is very hardy in most parts of Britain but it does like a sheltered position.

Camellia reticulata is a species from China, but gardeners generally grow the varieties and hybrids.

Here grown as free-standing shrubs in the medium to large size range, the beautiful hybrid 'Cornish Snow' massed with small white blooms (far left) is perfectly complemented by the equally attractive and very popular *Camellia × williamsii* 'Donation'.

These need to be in a greenhouse or conservatory, unless grown in mild parts of the country (the south-west) where they can be grown successfully out of doors. They make ideal wall shrubs in the south, given a warm sunny wall.

Flowers are freely produced in late winter and early spring, and the plants need plenty of sun to ripen the wood and to ensure good flowering. When grown in a greenhouse or conservatory, it is best to provide slight heat to keep out the frost, especially when the plants are in flower.

Height is 3m (10ft) plus, and spread 2.4-3.6m (8-12ft).

The varieties detailed on page 47 can be recommended.

Camellia saluenensis This species, from Western China, is one of the parents of the williamsii camellias. It is also an excellent plant in its own right, and is hardy, except in very cold or exposed areas, but is at its best grown against a wall.

The small single flowers are very freely produced in shades of pink, as well as white, mid-season. This species, which carries small deep green leaves, forms a large bush, of erect habit, to a height of 3m (10ft) or more, with a spread of 1.8m (6ft) plus in good conditions.

Camellia sasanqua comes from Japan and has scented autumn flowers set against small leaves. Gardeners generally grow the varieties.

These camellias need a warm aspect and protection from the frosts of autumn, which could damage the flowers. Flowering is best if the plants are grown in full sun, and they are particularly recommended for south or west facing walls.

Some varieties have fragrant flowers and they are generally single. Height and spread are in the region of 2.4-3m (8-10ft).

Recommended varieties are detailed on page 47.

FAR LEFT Single form of camellia, with one circle of flowers and a large cluster of stamens in the centre.
LEFT Formal double flowers are very neat and symmetrical, with many overlapping petals and no visible stamens.
BELOW FAR LEFT Anemone form flowers are so named because they really do resemble anemones.
BELOW LEFT Paeony forms can be either 'full' or 'loose' – as shown here.

CAMELLIAS FOR THE SPECIALIST

The camellias described in the previous pages are for general gardeners, but it may be that you are already a camellia enthusiast – or perhaps once you have started growing camellias you will become something of a collector of these plants, if you have sufficient space. Therefore, in this chapter I want to introduce a few of the camellia species (or wild plants) that are not widely grown but, I can assure you, are excellent plants.

You will not be able to buy these species from garden centres and nurseries, but they can be obtained from a specialist camellia grower. The several specialist growers in the U.K. produce catalogues that are well worth obtaining for all the information they contain, and the plants can be bought mail order. Indeed, from a large specialist, you will be able to buy all the camellias described in this book.

Please see page 17 for specialist growers particularly noted for their camellias.

To be absolutely honest, the species described here are not as spectacular as the camellias so far mentioned. But do all plants have to be flamboyant? I think not, for I, and many other gardeners, can appreciate subtle qualities in plants. And these species certainly have special qualities and attractions, and can provide a great deal of enjoyment when they are in flower.

The following, then, are some of the more easily grown species from the range available.

Camellia maliflora This species has small pink double flowers in the winter. Like many camellias, it is a native of China, and while it grows well enough on a warm sunny wall in the south of Britain, in most areas it is much happier in a cool greenhouse or conservatory. It is of modest stature, attaining a height of about 2.4m (8ft).

Camellia oleifera Another Chinese species, this time with single white flowers, slightly scented and produced in late autumn or early winter. It is a hardy species and presents no problem when grown out of doors in Britain.

Camellia sinensis As a nation of tea drinkers, surely the gardeners among us should have a tea plant – although not for procuring tea leaves, but for interest and the enjoyment of its small, white, fragrant flowers in winter. Again this is a Chinese shrub, but it can be grown out of doors in the mild south-west of Britain. In other parts of the country it is best grown in a greenhouse or conservatory. This is a low, compact, rounded shrub, with dull (that is, not shiny) deep green leaves.

Camellia × williamsii 'Elegant Beauty', a rose-pink paeony form that is ideal for providing colour on a north-facing wall. The flowers appear mid-season.

$C. \times williamsii$ hybrids: 'Anticipation', 'Bow Bells', 'Bowen Bryant', 'Brigadoon', 'Donation', 'Freedom Bell', 'Inspiration', 'J.C. Williams', 'Leonard Messel', and 'St. Ewe'.

Camellia japonica varieties: the pink or red varieties are best for growing outdoors.

Others: 'Cornish Snow'.

Camellias for growing against walls either as free-standing shrubs in front of a wall or actually trained to the wall:

North-facing wall: 'Cornish Snow'. The following williamsii hybrids – 'Bow Bells', 'Debbie', 'Donation', 'Elegant Beauty', 'Inspiration', 'J.C. Williams', 'November Pink', and 'St. Ewe'.

South-facing wall: *C. reticulata* varieties, like 'Dream Castle'. *C. sasanqua* varieties (see page 47).

East and west-facing walls: 'Cornish Snow'. Williamsii varieties 'Elegant Beauty' and 'November Pink'.

Another × *williamsii* variety, 'St. Ewe'. This very hardy single, of compact, upright habit, is also a good choice for north facing walls.

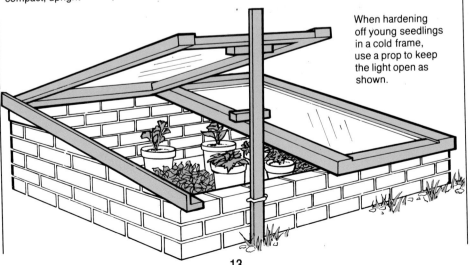

When hardening off young seedlings in a cold frame, use a prop to keep the light open as shown.

13

CAMELLIAS IN THE GARDEN

Camellias can be grown in shrub or mixed borders, and are superb subjects for woodland gardens. It is recommended that other plants are grown with them, rather than growing the camellias in isolation, for then colour and interest are assured when the camellias have finished flowering.

Although camellias have attractive foliage, when they are not in flower there will be just a mass of greenery, and I feel that this needs relieving with other plants.

However, be careful in your choice of plants to associate with camellias for by no means all plants look 'right'. As camellias can only be grown in acid or lime-free soils, it is best to choose companion plants which like the same conditions.

Companion plants Rhododendrons of all kinds (including winter flowering ones) associate well with camellias. Also consider the dwarf evergreen azaleas which bloom in late spring/early summer, and the deciduous azaleas which flower in summer.

Magnolias are natural companions for camellias, and although many make large specimens, there is a delightful small grower for limited space – the star magnolia (*M. stellata*) with it's white starry blooms in spring.

For mild areas the evergreen, white-flowered eucryphias are a good choice, if you have space for large shrubs. For sheltered positions try the pieris, with evergreen foliage and flowers like lily of the valley. They make fairly large shrubs, and some, like 'Flame of the Forest', have brilliant red young leaves.

There are many other beautiful shrubs that make good companions for camellias. I cannot leave out the winter-flowering witch hazels (hamamelis) with their yellow, gold

LEFT 'Donation' with its large pink blooms is teamed with *Rhododendron* 'Brocade' and, in the foreground, Azalea 'Hatsu-giri'.
RIGHT A vigorous, free-flowering *C. japonica* variety.
BELOW A wall-trained variety of *Camellia reticulata*.

Heaths and heathers are excellent ground-cover plants, provided they receive plenty of sun. For summer flowering there are many varieties of the ling (*Calluna vulgaris*), while for winter colour choose varieties of the winter heath (*Erica carnea*).

Many bulbs and perennial plants look 'right' with camellias, including lilies, miniature cyclamen, the candelabra primulas (such as varieties of *Primula japonica*), and the drumstick primrose (*Primula denticulata*), blue poppies (meconopsis) and plantain lilies (hostas).

or orange spidery flowers on bare branches, nor the winter-flowering Cornelian cherry (*Cornus mas*) with masses of yellow blooms that come before the new leaves.

For autumn leaf colour the Japanese maples (varieties of *Acer palmatum* and *A. japonicum*), really show up well against a background of camellia foliage.

Consider also some low-growing plants to provide ground cover around the camellias. Do not plant them too close, however, for camellias have shallow roots and even a slight disturbance of the surrounding soil could damage them.

CAMELLIA HEDGES

Some camellias can be grown as informal or formal hedges and screens, particularly those with very dense or bushy upright growth. Some are listed below.

For informal hedges (varieties that need little or no clipping)
- 'Anticipation' (williamsii hybrid)
- 'E.G. Waterhouse' (williamsii hybrid)
- 'Yours Truly' (japonica variety)

For formal hedges (varieties that will need some trimming)
- 'Joseph Pfingstl' (japonica variety)
- 'Tiptoe' (williamsii hybrid)

15

CHOOSING QUALITY PLANTS

There are now several ways of buying camellias – by visiting garden centres and nurseries and selecting plants yourself; by ordering plants from a mail order specialist camellia grower. Or, you can buy from certain high street chain stores, but with a very limited choice.

Always buy from a reputable nurseryman or from a garden centre with a reputation for quality plants. The advantage of buying from a garden centre is that you can see plants in flower, choose those that appeal to you and plant immediately. Plants are sold in pots or other containers (this includes mail order plants) and therefore establish much better than root-balled plants.

When buying from a garden centre or nursery it is, of course, up to you to ensure that you buy good-quality plants. The following tips on what you should look for will help you to choose plants of quality.

• Avoid very small plants as they are difficult to establish.
• Avoid excessively large plants, for the same reason.
• Ideal plants are in the region of 45-60cm (18-24in) in height, and up to a maximum of 1.2m (4ft) high.
• Plants should be well-branched from the ground up, and have plenty of flower buds.
• The foliage should be fresh-looking, green and healthy. Avoid plants with leaves that are yellowing, or wind-scorched.
• Avoid plants with yellow mottling on the leaves as this may be a virus.
• Plants should be well-established in their pots, but not pot-bound (pot tightly packed with roots) or loose in their pots.
• The compost must be moist: not dry or saturated with moisture.
• Each plant should be labelled with the name of the variety.

• Buy only plants that have been well hardened off – rather than plants with soft lush growth straight from a greenhouse (unless they are specifically intended for greenhouse cultivation).

Buying from a specialist grower
For the widest selection of varieties you will need to buy from a specialist camellia grower – by mail order if you cannot make a personal visit.

Remember that a specialist can help you to select varieties for particular areas or situations.

The first step is to send for a catalogue giving information on the varieties available and their suitability for particular areas and situations. You can rely on a specialist to supply good-quality plants, and they will be correctly labelled.

A young *Camellia × williamsii*, 'Anticipation', already showing the hallmarks of a healthy, well-established plant. Well-shaped, glossy leaves, and a very good display of flowers.

THE FOLLOWING ARE NOTED FOR CAMELLIAS:

• James Trehane and Sons Ltd, Stapehill Road, Hampreston, Wimborne, Dorset, BH21 7NE. (Phone: 0202 873490). The famous camellia specialist, with a very comprehensive and detailed catalogue.

• Exbury Gardens Ltd, Exbury, near Southampton, SO4 1AZ. (Phone: 0703 891203). Noted for camellias and other choice plants. You will have to visit and buy from the plant centre, but a list of plants is available.

• Bodnant Garden Nursery, Tal-y-Cafn, Colwyn Bay, North Wales, LL28 5RE. (Phone: 049 267 460). Noted for camellias and other choice plants. A list is available.

Buying from chain stores It is now possible to buy camellias from some high street chain stores and these are sold when in flower as house plants. However, the camellia does not make a good houseplant, although you could keep it indoors while it is in flower, if you make sure the plant does not suffer in any way. This means keeping it in a very cool airy room in really good light. If you cannot provide these conditions, plant it immediately in the garden or, if necessary, first harden it off in a cold frame.

When buying plants from a chain store, bear in mind the tips already given as regards quality. But you are obviously not going to have a very wide choice of plants.

Another of the hardy × *williamsii* varieties, 'Inspiration', having attained a good height and clearly flourishing as an eye-catching frontispiece to a brick-built house. One word of caution: beware of the soil drying out quickly in this kind of location, particularly during the summer months.

GROWING CAMELLIAS

Camellias can be grown outdoors all over Britain but you must choose kinds suited to the climate in your area, as indicated in the descriptive lists. There is little point in growing outdoors in cold areas varieties whose buds could be killed by frosts. Camellias need warmth and a humid atmosphere (provided by rainfall) to ripen their new growth. This is no problem in some parts of Britain, but more difficult in others.

As a basic guide, camellias need shade for part of the day in areas of low humidity. In areas of high humidity plants can be grown in sunny spots.

The north-east is a difficult area because it has low rainfall and therefore low humidity, cool temperatures in summer and often very cold conditions in winter. In such an area try to find a warm sheltered spot, with shade from the sun for part of the day (known as a micro-climate).

In the south-east, rainfall is somewhat higher, and both summer and winter temperatures are higher. However, I still consider it best to plant camellias in partial shade.

Many western areas are very favourable for growing camellias out of doors, and gardeners in Cornwall, for example, have perfect conditions. Humidity is high and the climate mild. Choose well-sheltered planting sites in the sun.

Type of shade This should always be light, as camellias need good light. Aim for a combination of sun and light or dappled shade. Avoid very heavy shade.

Tall trees, with a high canopy of branches, provide very good conditions. They give sufficient shade to protect the leaves from very hot mid-day sun without blocking it out completely.

Soils and their improvement Ideally, soil should be light rather than heavy (for example, sandy types or light to medium loams).

Soil must be acid or lime free. Before planting, carry out a soil test, using one of the inexpensive soil-testing kits available at most garden centres. If the reading shows a pH of between 4.5 and 6.5, camellias will thrive, for the soil's condition is acid.

All soils must be prepared well before planting, by double digging the site (that is, to two depths of the spade).

Add plenty of sphagnum peat, leafmould or 'Forest Bark' to each trench during digging. As a rough guide, use about half a barrowload to each 1.21m (4ft) width of trench. Mix it well into the topsoil also, as there must be a high level of humus or organic matter present to give plants a good start.

The soil must be well drained, too. Drainage can often be improved by digging in plenty of coarse sand or grit (these must be lime free).

THINGS TO AVOID
- Early morning sun will rapidly thaw out frozen flower buds, damaging or even killing them.
- Draughts. Camellias hate cold draughts, though ordinary wind is no problem. Try to find a sheltered spot.
- Frost pockets. These are very low-lying areas (such as the bottom of a valley) into which cold air drains and frost collects. Frosts can damage or kill flower buds.

Whatever medium you use for the supporting wall, do ensure efficient drainage, as necessary.

If the bed is built directly on to the existing soil, drainage should not be a problem.

Wooden logs, laid one on top of another, or side by side, should be treated with preservative.

BUILDING A RAISED BED

If your soil is very badly drained and cannot be improved, you could grow camellias in a raised bed, about 60cm (2ft) deep.

● Build it up with logs, walling blocks or bricks.

● Build it direct on to the soil.

● Fill the 'frame' with a lime-free compost, such as ericaceous compost (available from garden centres).

Off to a good start In theory, camellias in containers can be planted at any time of year providing the soil is neither very wet nor frozen. But best establishment is obtained when the soil is warm, which really rules out the winter period. To my mind, the optimum periods for planting are late spring or early autumn. Summer planting is fine provided you do not let plants suffer from dry conditions.

If you cannot plant immediately, perhaps because the time of the year or soil conditions are unsuitable, keep the plants cold until you can. The pots should be plunged to their rims in soil in a spot sheltered from cold winds. This treatment will prevent the compost in the pots from becoming frozen or rapidly drying out. Never allow the compost to dry out before planting as this severely sets back the plants, and results in leaf and flower bud drop.

Even the vigorous and free-flowering *Camellia × williamsii* 'Donation', popular for its hardiness as well as for its stunning orchid pink blooms is all the better for a little protection. Here it flourishes in a shrub border shielded from wind by a hedge.

How to plant Before planting camellias in the previously dug and prepared soil (see page 18) apply fertilizer and prick it into the surface, using a fork. I can recommend 'Verdley' Soil Conditioning Growmore or John Innes base fertilizer, applied at about 113g per sq. m (4oz per sq. yd).

When planting container-grown camellias in well-prepared soil, all you need do is to take out a planting hole as deep as, and slightly wider than, the rootball. Place the plant in the centre of the hole, and check that when planting is complete the top of the rootball will be level with the surrounding soil. It is a great mistake to plant camellias too deeply.

Then work fine soil between the rootball and the side of the hole, firming it with a heel as you proceed. Finally, firm thoroughly all around the plant; this is essential.

If the camellia is pot bound (so that the pot is tightly packed with roots), before planting carefully tease out the main coiled roots and spread them out in the hole, working fine soil around and between them to ensure good establishment.

If the plant is fairly tall you may find that it needs support from a stout bamboo cane. Insert this before filling in the planting hole, to avoid accidentally damaging the roots. Tie in the main stem with soft garden string.

After planting, mulch with peat or 'Forest Bark' – for full details of mulching, please see page 22.

Keep newly planted camellias well watered in dry weather as they must not be allowed to dry out. For more details please see page 22.

Transplanting larger plants Over the years I have received a lot of letters from gardeners asking if they can move camellias some years after planting, either because they find that their plants are in the wrong place, or they wish to take the plants with them when moving house.

It is possible to move established plants up to about 2m (6ft) in height. Any larger, though, and special lifting equipment would be needed, as there would be a large, heavy rootball.

Ideally, move established plants in early autumn. Start by digging a

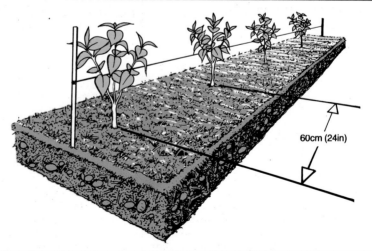

When planting a camellia hedge, use young plants no more than 60cm (24in) high and plant them spaced 60cm (24in) apart in a single line. Then water them well in. The planting site would need to be a strip of about 1.2m (4ft) in width.

60cm (24in)

RIGHT *Camellia japonica* 'Jupiter', with its abundance of large crimson-red blooms makes a spectacular screen and here enjoys the shade provided by the trees beyond.
BELOW RIGHT A close-up of 'Jupiter', clearly showing the single form of the flowerheads on this old variety.

trench all around the plant, to just beyond the leaf spread, and about 45cm (18in) deep.

Then use a spade to cut underneath the plant until it is completely loosened, but the roots are still surrounded by a ball of soil. This must be kept intact so tightly wrap the ball in a sheet of polythene or hessian before lifting the plant out of the hole. Only remove the wrap when the plant is actually standing in its new planting hole.

Planting a camellia hedge Young plants, about 45-60cm (18-24in) high, should be planted in a single line, 60cm (24in) apart, to form a hedge.

The planting site for the hedge can be a 1-1.2m (3-4ft) wide strip of land, thoroughly prepared as described on page 18.

Feeding the plants I do not recommend feeding camellias with animal manures, because these are too rich and can cause root problems such as root burn. Nevertheless they do need feeding each spring with the major nutrients or foods: nitrogen, phosphorous and potash. The minor nutrients such as magnesium, manganese and iron are generally found in the soil in sufficient quantity, but you will need to apply a compound fertilizer containing nitrogen, phosphorous and potash, such as 'Verdley' Soil Conditioning Growmore.

Apply this fertilizer in early spring, according to the instructions on the pack. Usually these entail simply sprinkling it over the soil surface. Do not fork it in or this may damage the roots of the camellias.

21

I find that plants benefit from further nitrogen applied to the soil in late spring, so I give a dressing of sulphate of ammonia, at 28g per sq. m (1oz per sq. yd).

In early summer, to encourage the production of flower buds, and to assist growth generally, I apply superphosphate (supplies phosphorous) and Epsom salts (supplying magnesium), both at 28g per sq. m (1oz per sq. yd). Fertilizers should be applied only when the soil is moist, so if the ground is dry first water it thoroughly and allow time for the plants to become fully charged with water before applying the fertilizer.

Watering It is essential to water camellias in dry weather, particularly newly planted specimens, but established plants also. The soil can dry out very rapidly under large trees and shrubs, so keep a careful watch on these areas.

If plants are allowed to dry out flower buds may not be produced, or may drop before they have chance to open. This applies equally to young and well-established plants.

It is best to use rainwater if your tapwater is 'hard' or alkaline, and water when the soil is just becoming dry on the surface but before it becomes too dry lower down. Always give the soil a good soaking at each watering; provided you have soft tap water, this is best achieved by using a garden sprinkler on the end of a hosepipe.

Mulching Camellias, like many other shrubs, benefit greatly from mulching with a 5cm (2in) deep layer of organic matter spread over the surface of the soil, around and between the plants, to cover the root area. In practice, an entire bed or border is mulched, rather than individual plants within the bed.

The benefits of mulching are:
• It prevents the soil from drying out rapidly – and this is particularly important when you are growing camellias.
• A mulch prevents the growth of annual weeds; although it will not suppress invasive perennial weeds such as dandelions, docks and couch grass.
• The organic matter supplies beneficial humus to the soil.

Several materials can be used for mulching, but among the best for camellias is pulverized and composted bark, namely 'Forest Bark'. This takes a long time to rot down completely, so the mulch is very long-lasting.

Camellias make truly spectacular shrubs when well cared for, and that means – above all – ensuring an adequate water supply during dry spells. The rewards for such pampering are well worth the effort as can be seen in these pictures. The ever popular 'Donation' (above right), and the aristocratic 'Contessa Lavinia Maggi' (right). Both are prized varieties.

HOW MUCH WATER TO APPLY

Apply sufficient water to penetrate the soil to a depth of at least 15cm (6in). To ensure this, you need to apply the equivalent of 2.5cm (1in) of rain, which means in practice applying 27 litres per sq. m (4¾ galls. per sq. yd).

Peat is also an excellent mulch around camellias; use either sphagnum peat or the darker coloured sedge peat. Or, if you are able to obtain leafmould, use this for mulching as it is just as good as peat.

Mulch camellias immediately after planting, and mulch established plants every spring – remembering to do this only when the soil is thoroughly moist. If necessary,

water heavily first; allow the surface to drain before laying the mulch loosely – do not firm it down. One of the problems with a mulch is that birds often scratch around in it, scattering that nearest the edge of a bed over paths and lawns. So you may need to tidy it up occasionally.

Weed control It is essential to keep weeds under control, as dense weeds can seriously retard the growth of young camellias, robbing them of foods and moisture.

There are various ways of controlling weeds among camellias. Many gardeners pull them out by hand. On no account hoe or fork them out, for camellia roots are very near the soil surface and could be damaged; leave the soil completely undisturbed.

Mulching will suppress annual weeds, but not perennial ones. To control these you will need to use a suitable chemical weedkiller such as glyphosate.

If you do not mulch, you will also need to control annual weeds by hand, or use chemical weedkillers.

To kill existing annual weeds I can recommend 'Weedol', which contains paraquat and is best used in spring, summer or autumn. It can be applied with a watering can fitted with a dribble bar, making sure you thoroughly wet the growth of weeds, but on no account let it come in contact with the foliage of the camellias, or it will scorch the leaves.

Once the soil is free from weeds I would suggest that you use the weedkiller simazine to prevent the germination of further weed seeds and keep the soil weed free for many months. Use only on weed-free soil. Simazine can be applied in spring, and maybe again in the autumn, using a watering can fitted with a dribble bar as before.

PRUNING

Unlike many other ornamental shrubs, camellias need little pruning. They are truly labour-saving plants. However, a little attention may be needed, as outlined below, to enjoy them growing at their best.

Eventually, as the plants become large, there may be some dead wood to remove, particularly in the centre of the bushes where there is little light. Removal of dead wood should be carried out in the winter, cutting it back to live wood or to the main stems. If dead wood is not removed it may become diseased, and the problem could spread to healthy wood.

Any overlong shoots which spoil the shape of the bush can be cut back in summer, immediately above a growth bud.

Sometimes, young plants tend to be leggy and should be pruned back in late winter before the buds break. If left, they will become bare at the base, whereas we want bushy growth from ground level.

Very old plants which you consider are too large can be cut back severely in late winter – virtually to ground level. They will then make new growth and bush out.

Sometimes shoots become frosted and die back. In this instance cut them back to live wood, immediately above a growth bud. The best time for this is when buds have started into growth.

Always use very sharp secateurs for pruning, as ragged cuts must be avoided. Clean cuts heal much more quickly and are less likely to become infected by diseases.

Large pruning cuts – say 2.5cm (1in) and over – should be sealed with a pruning compound to prevent entry of diseases and moisture.

Camellia japonica 'Elegans', is noteworthy for its large, anemone form, rose-pink blooms, but its spreading habit of growth may eventually call for a little pruning. Also, *japonica* varieties tend to hang on to their blooms so you may need to remove dead flowers by hand. Even so, this is an excellent shrub.

A 'formal' hedge in need of correct shaping.

This wedge shape will give weather protection.

The obliging *Camellia × williamsii* 'J.C. Williams' and 'Donation' (right), do not usually need dead-heading.

Dead flowers Do not leave dead flowers on the bushes because when they turn brown they look unsightly. They will usually fall off if you simply shake the branches, but if this does not work pick them off individually.

Some camellias obligingly drop their dead blooms and this applies especially to varieties of *C. × williamsii*, *C. reticulata* and *C. sasanqua*. However, most varieties of *C. japonica* hang on to their dead blooms and must be attended to after flowering.

If buds or blooms are killed by frost, again they must be removed. A very good reason for not growing these magnificent flowering shrubs in frost pockets!

Trimming a camellia hedge Most of the camellias I have recommended for use as hedging do not need clipping to keep them neat, compact and dense. However, some do need trimming and this is best carried out as soon as flowering is over (see above).

If you are growing a formal hedge, train it to a wedge shape – that is, wider at the base than at the top. The sides should gradually taper inwards to the top. This shape ensures that the hedge sheds snow; if snow collects at the top it can split a hedge apart.

Always trim the hedge with secateurs, not electric trimmers or shears, which cut leaves in half, making them very unsightly.

CAMELLIAS IN CONTAINERS

Camellias grow extremely well in ornamental pots and tubs, and it is an ideal way of growing them if you have an alkaline (limy or chalky) soil; or otherwise unsuitable conditions such as waterlogging in winter. One can provide perfect conditions in containers. There are many other very good reasons for growing them in this way too. Read on!

• It is an excellent way of growing camellias if you have only a small paved garden with no soil beds or borders.

• Growing in pots and tubs enables you to move plants around. For example, they can be taken into a greenhouse or conservatory to flower, and moved out again after flowering.

• Pots and tubs containing camellias are ideal for decorating paved areas of the garden, such as patios and terraces. When the plants have finished flowering the pots can be moved to another part of the garden, if desired, to be replaced by other colourful plants.

• When grown in pots and tubs, camellias can be placed in the most suitable aspect as regards sun, shade and shelter.

• It is very easy to grow camellias in containers. No special skills are needed – the only requirements are a suitable compost and efficient drainage.

• Many plants can be grown in a comparatively small space, enabling you to build up a good collection of different varieties to spread the season of flowering.

• The pots and tubs of camellias can be used as focal points in a garden, particularly when they are in full flower.

• Even large pots and tubs are not difficult to move if you use a sack trolley. This is a good investment if you have a large garden, as it can also be used to move other heavy objects around, such as sacks of fertilizer or compost, rocks, paving slabs and so on.

Types of container Go to any large garden centre and you will find a wide range of ornamental containers on sale. Some of them however, are not suitable for camellia culture because they are too shallow. Containers for camellias should be in the region of 45-60cm (18-24in) deep. The diameter will depend on the size of plant, but more of this when I discuss planting and potting on (see pages 28-30).

In my opinion ornamental containers should complement, not detract from the beauty of the plants. For this very good reason, wherever possible they should be made of natural products; avoid highly coloured or patterned pots and tubs.

• Terra-cotta. This is my first choice. Terra-cotta pots and tubs are made from clay and are a beautiful warm orange – the colour of traditional flower pots. There is a good selection available, from very large pots to urn shapes. Some are of the style that one sees in Mediterranean gardens, and very good they look, too, on a patio or terrace.

• Wooden tubs. My second choice and, again, a natural product. It is possible to buy used tubs (barrels that have been cut down), or purpose-made wooden tubs in various shades, from dark to light brown. Take care, however, to buy an untreated tub, because if a caustic preservative such as creosote has been used, it could be disastrous. Instead, treat the tub yourself with a preservative such as Cuprinol wood preservative.

• Modern concrete tubs can look attractive if they are of a neutral colour, and they're very durable.

FAR LEFT *Camellia japonica* 'Adolphe Audusson', a first-class, compact shrub.
LEFT CENTRE *C. saluensis* varieties make medium to large shrubs. Check with the nursery before container planting.
LEFT *C. reticulata* 'Captain Rawes' – the initially trumpet-shaped flowers open full out in time.
ABOVE *C. × williamsii* 'St. Ewe', a single cup form.

Establishing Plants The most important consideration when growing camellias in pots and tubs is the compost, for it must be acid or free from lime and chalk. Potting composts are used, and they can be soilless or soil-based. So the decision regarding which one to use is simply a matter of personal preference.

Soilless composts consist of peat and sand, with fertilizers added, and are very light in weight. They are taking over from traditional soil-based composts (see right).

Soilless composts are sold in garden centres in various-size packs. The ones to choose for camellias are the ericaceous composts, specially formulated for lime-hating plants.

Soil-based composts are heavier than soilless composts and there is less likelihood of plants blowing over when these are used. Use John Innes potting compost but as most of these contain chalk, do ask for an acid mix. If acid J.I. is not available, use soilless ericaceous.

Home-made compost. I have made up a compost at home for camellias, and have found it to be very good. It consists mainly of peat and leafmould, with the addition of coarse lime-free sand. A little acid loam (soil) can also be included if you can buy it from a garden centre. A rough guide would be: 7 parts peat and leafmould, 3 parts coarse, lime-free sand and 2 parts acid loam.

LEFT *Camellia* × *williamsii* 'Brigadoon' is a very hardy shrub in all parts of Britain. BELOW *C. sasanqua* 'Tricolor', a striking single form – white striped with pink and red.

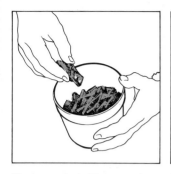

Start your plant off in a container only slightly larger than the rootball; supply adequate drainage in the form of crocks.

Cover crocks with a thin layer of peat. Add a layer of good quality compost and firm down well with the flat of your fingers.

Stand plant on the layer of compost. Gradually sprinkle in more compost between the roots. Firm in as before.

Planting It is not advisable to plant a young camellia immediately into a large tub or pot because there will be too large a volume of compost around the roots. This is inclined to remain too wet as it will not be permeated with roots, and therefore roots may rot, resulting in the death of the plant. So choose a container only slightly larger than the rootball of the new plant.

Initial potting on of a young 45-60cm (18-24in) high plant in, say, a 12.5cm (5in) pot, as bought from a garden centre, should be into a 17cm (7in) pot.

I prefer to carry out potting as soon as flowering is over, which will be some time in the spring, according to the variety being grown.

I put a layer of drainage material in the bottom of the pot or tub, for example, crocks or broken clay flower pots (do make sure that there are drainage holes in the container). Cover the crocks with a thin layer of rough peat followed by a layer of compost, which should be firmed. Then stand the plant on this and work compost down between the rootball and the sides of the container, firming it as you go with your fingers.

When using potting composts, I would strongly advise reading the manufacturer's instructions on the pack, for some need more firming than others. As a general rule, soil-less composts need minimum firming, while soil-based types need moderate firming.

After potting, give a thorough watering to settle the compost.

AFTERCARE OF CONTAINER PLANTS

Once a pot is full of roots, but before it becomes really tightly packed (when a plant is then said to be 'pot bound'), move on the plant to a larger sized container. So a camellia that you first settled in a 17cm (7in) pot would be moved into a 22cm (9in) pot; and from there to a 30cm (12in) container. Thereafter the plant can go into quite a large tub or pot, say 45cm (18in) in diameter, or maybe 60cm (24in).

I know of some people who *have* put a young camellia straight into a large container with successful results, which shows that there are no hard and fast rules in gardening. But I would recommend the little-by-little approach, and using the composts recommended on the previous page.

Fresh compost Plants in final containers will need top dressing with fresh compost each spring. Scrape off a little of the old compost, taking care not to go too deeply or you may damage the roots. Then replace with a layer of fresh compost, using the same type that the plant is already growing in.

When a plant has been in its final container for several years you will need to replace much more of the old, worn-out compost, to keep the plant in good condition.

First remove the plant from its container. Then tease away about 5cm (2in) of the old compost from the sides, bottom and top of the rootball to make it smaller.

Then, using fresh compost, repot the plant into the same container, after cleaning it. The potting procedure is the same as already described on the previous page.

Feeding Feed camellias from mid-spring to late summer, at monthly intervals, using granular and liquid fertilizers.

From mid-spring to early summer I use a fertilizer which has a high proportion of nitrogen, such as Rose 'Plus'. It also contains phosphorous, potash and magnesium.

Each spring, scrape off a little of the top compost, taking care not to damage any of the roots.

Use replacement compost of the same type as that in which the plant is already growing.

When compost is level with soil mark on the plant, firm well in with your fingers; then water.

TOP *Camellia ×
williamsii* 'Debbie',
with rose-pink
flowers.

ABOVE *C. japonica*
'Lady Vansittart',
healthy growth in a
container.

From mid-summer to late summer I use a fertilizer which has a high proportion of potash, but which is low in nitrogen, for example, Liquid Tomato 'Plus' (there is no reason why you should not use a tomato fertilizer for other plants).

When using these fertilizers follow the manufacturer's instructions. Do not feed camellias after late summer or you will harm the plants.

Watering With camellias one must avoid extremes of moisture in the compost. The compost must not be allowed to dry out, and it must not be kept very wet.

● Drying out results in loss of flower buds.

● Very wet conditions cause yellowing of the leaves, which eventually drop; root rot; and eventual death of the plant.

Do not use a 'hard' or alkaline water. If your tapwater is hard it is advisable to collect and use rainwater for your camellias.

Insulation of pots Roots must not be allowed to freeze. If the compost freezes solid the roots will be killed, so insulate the containers in autumn and winter by wrapping them thickly with dry straw or bracken, which can be held in place with a piece of galvanized wire netting wrapped around the container.

31

CAMELLIAS IN THE GREENHOUSE

Plants in containers can be flowered in a greenhouse or conservatory, including varieties of *C. japonica, C. × williamsii,* and *C. reticulata.* There is no doubt that one achieves much better quality blooms under glass as they are protected from the weather. However, most camellias do not need to be kept under glass all the year round. In fact, I house the plants in autumn, where they flower in the winter and spring, usually earlier than outside.

The ideal temperature to maintain is 4.5-10°C (40-50°F). However, an unheated greenhouse or conservatory would also be suitable, but even here I would suggest a little heat in really severe weather to keep out the frost. Try to keep out frost when the flowers are opening, and at the other extreme, avoid very high temperatures when the plants are in flower.

When conditions are cool keep the air dry, but in warm conditions, such as we may experience in spring, increase humidity by damping down the floor with water.

Ensure good ventilation at all times as camellias hate a stagnant,

RIGHT *Camellia ×
williamsii* 'Inspiration'
flourishing under
glass.

LEFT Many varieties
of camellia are
suitable for growing in
a greenhouse or
conservatory. And
most can be safely set
outside in the warmer
months, if they're
easily movable.

stuffy atmosphere. Also ensure maximum light, but in the spring (and in summer if the plants are still in the house) shade from strong sunshine.

At all times the compost should be kept steadily moist but not wet.

After flowering I put the plants outside in the spring when they have finished flowering, but I wait until the frosts are over to prevent the soft young growth from being damaged. Frosting will set back the plants and there is a strong possibility that fewer flower buds will be formed.

To prevent the compost from drying out very rapidly during the summer, I stand the plants in a plunge bed, easily made on a spare piece of ground. Simply form a timber framework on the ground, slightly higher than the pots. Then spread a thin layer of well-weathered ashes or sand over the bottom, stand the pots in the frame and fill in between them with more ashes or sand, up to the rims of the pots.

The camellias should be in a sheltered, semi-shaded position. Keep the compost steadily moist throughout the growing season and feed the plants as described on page 21.

Permanent residents If you are fortunate enough to have a large greenhouse or conservatory then camellias can be planted permanently in soil beds or borders, prepared as described for outdoor cultivation (see page 18).

Obviously, even in a large greenhouse or conservatory, space is limited and so the plants will need regular pruning to prevent them from becoming too large. After flowering each year cut back the branches to side shoots lower down. Do not be too severe – just sufficient to contain the plants within the space that is available for them.

MAKING MORE PLANTS

You may wish to increase some of your camellias, so I will now detail the various methods of propagation. Probably the easiest methods for the amateur gardener are stem cuttings, leaf-bud cuttings and seeds. Grafting requires greater skill, but more advanced gardeners may like to try.

Stem cuttings Cuttings produce bushier plants than grafted specimens and this is another reason for strongly recommending this method of propagation.

Some varieties root more easily than others, but most varieties of *C. japonica* and *C. sasanqua* root well from stem cuttings. I would recommend that you try cuttings of any varieties you have to see what the result is.

Take cuttings in late summer or early autumn, using semi-ripe shoots produced in the current year (shoots that are hard and woody at the base but still soft and green at the top).

The cuttings should be about 15cm (6in) long and consist of three nodes (leaf joints). Cut immediately below a node at the base, and immediately above a node at the top. The base of each cutting should be 'wounded' by removing a slice of bark about 2.5cm (1in) long, to encourage rooting. Then dip the base of each cutting in 'Keriroot' hormone rooting powder.

Insert each cutting in its own pot of lime-free potting compost, which is formulated for cuttings, etc. Then place the pots in a heated propagating case with a temperature of 21°C (70°F) until roots form.

Overwinter the rooted cuttings in a cool greenhouse and pot them on in the spring, first removing the top 5-7.5cm (2-3in) of growth to ensure well-branched plants.

Grow on the young plants in a greenhouse, feeding them as described earlier, until they are 45-60cm (18-24in) high. Then harden off the plants in a cold frame before planting them out. It takes approximately 20 to 21 months to produce a plant of good size for planting out.

Take cuttings of semi-ripe shoots. Cut just below a 'base' node, just above a 'top' node.

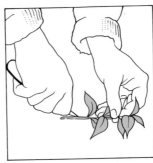

At the base of each cutting, remove a slice of bark to encourage the rooting process.

Insert the wounded end of each cutting into hormone rooting powder before planting.

Leaf-bud cuttings This is a useful technique if cutting material is limited, as the cuttings are comparatively small. Leaf-bud cuttings are taken at the same time as stem cuttings, using the same type of material.

Each cutting consists of one leaf with a bud in the axil, plus a portion of stem about 3.5cm (1½in) long. The leaf should be at the top of the stem.

Once the cuttings have been prepared and dipped in hormone rooting powder, they are treated in the same way as stem cuttings. Insert them so that the bud in the leaf axil is just above compost level.

Grafting This is a useful method if propagation material is limited – for instance, if you have only small plants with relatively few shoots. It is also useful if you want to propagate varieties that prove difficult to root from cuttings.

It is possible to produce 60cm (24in) high plants in one year from grafting, but they will not be as bushy as those raised from cuttings.

Grafting involves joining together parts of two plants. A piece of stem of the variety to be propagated (known as a scion) is joined on to part of another plant (known as a rootstock) that provides the root system of the new plant.

Camellias are grafted in mid-autumn. The rootstock should be an 18 month old seedling of *C. japonica*, well established in a 15cm (6in) pot. Either grow the seedlings yourself, as described on page 36, or buy from a shrub nurseryman. When grafting, the compost in the pot should be on the dry side, so allow it to partially dry out a few days before commencing.

The scion is prepared from a current year's shoot, and it should be about 20cm (8in) long. The scion is bound tightly on to the rootstock with a strip of plastic tape.

The graft shown overleaf is the side graft (but other types can also be used for camellias), because this is a fairly easy one for amateurs and can be very clearly explained by the use of a diagram. However, do bear in mind that the width and length of the cut on the scion should match exactly the width and length of the cut on the rootstock, otherwise the graft may not 'take' or unite. Also,

When making leaf bud cuttings, use the same type of material as selected for stem cuttings.

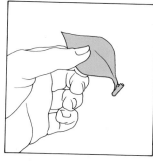
You will need a leaf with a bud in its axil, together with a 3.5cm (1½in) length of stem.

After treating the cutting with rooting powder, plant with the bud just above the surface.

use a very sharp knife to ensure very clean, smooth cuts, or again you may not have a successful union.

Once you have completed the grafting, place the pot in a heated propagating case with high humidity and a temperature of 21°C (70°F). Without these conditions, the graft may not 'take'. From now on keep the compost in the pot moist.

When the graft has united – it could take up to eight weeks – remove the pot from the propagating case and carefully remove the tape. An indication that the graft has taken is the scion starting into growth.

Grow on the young plant in a greenhouse as described for young plants raised from cuttings.

Plants from seeds It is good fun raising plants from seeds but I should add that the seedlings may not resemble their parents when they come into flower, except in the case of species.

Seeds of some varieties are not fertile and therefore will not grow, so that may account for non-germination.

Camellia seeds should be harvested in the autumn and sown immediately. If kept for several months they may not germinate.

The method I use is to mix the seeds with a quantity of moist peat and place this mixture in a clear polythene bag. The top of the bag should then be tied, before placing it in a warm spot indoors – for many people this would be an airing cupboard.

I find that the seeds germinate within about two months. You can actually see many of them germinating. When the roots are about 5cm (2in) long, remove the seedlings and pot them individually into small pots, only lightly covering the actual

seed. From now onwards the seedlings should be grown on in a greenhouse, treating them in the same way as young plants from cuttings. The only difference is that seedlings generally take about five years to flower, so you will need plenty of patience.

Grafting is done in the autumn. Here, a side cut is made in a rootstock of *C. japonica*. A 20cm (8in) long scion from a current year's shoot is cut to match exactly, and inserted into the cut. The scion is then held in position while bound into place with a length of garden twine or a plastic strip.

36

PESTS AND DISEASES

A number of pests and diseases can affect camellias, although in the main they stay very healthy. So you will not be forever spraying your plants. The foes that I consider most important are described below, together with methods of controlling them. As soon as any trouble is noticed, do take steps to control it, for if pests and diseases are allowed to build up, they can have a very debilitating effect on plants.

PESTS

Aphids These are greenfly and their relations, but it is generally a brown aphid that attacks camellias, clustering around shoot tips and distorting the leaves by sap sucking. Green aphids may appear under glass in the spring. Whatever their colour, all aphids secrete a sticky honeydew, on which grows an unsightly fungus called sooty mould. As soon as aphids are noticed spray plants with 'Rapid' Greenfly Killer.

Scale insects These are immobile, shield-shaped or rounded insects found on the stems and the undersides of leaves, where they suck the sap. When they are noticed, spray plants with 'Sybol' 2.

Vine weevils The adult weevil is a black, beetle-like creature with a long snout, and eats notches out of the leaf edges. The larvae or grubs live in soil or compost and eat roots. To eradicate adults spray plants with 'Sybol' 2, and to combat larvae drench compost with 'Sybol' 2.

DISEASES

Honey fungus This fungal disease can rapidly kill camellias and many other shrubs and trees. Black, bootlace-like threads spread through the soil and infect roots; white fungal threads grow under the bark; and honey-coloured toadstools grow around the base of trunk or stems. If a plant suddenly seems to be ailing, perhaps with branches dying back for no apparent reason, then suspect honey fungus. You may be able to save the shrub by heavily drenching the soil around it with 'Clean-Up'. If the shrub dies, dig it out, burn it and drench the hole with 'Clean-Up'.

Leaf spot Brown or grey disease spots appear on leaves, due to excess humidity under glass and airless conditions, so keep the air drier and increase ventilation. Spray the plants with 'Benlate'.

Virus-like diseases These may cause yellow mottling or spotting on leaves and are transmitted by aphids and during propagation. So keep aphids under control, and do not propagate from plants showing these symptoms. Generally this trouble is not serious and plants can be left. There is no control.

PHYSIOLOGICAL DISORDERS

Physiological disorders are not diseases but are caused by incorrect cultivation or unsuitable conditions.

Bud drop Can be caused by too much feeding, by applying too much nitrogen late in the growing period, and by compost or soil drying out.

Yellow leaves Can be caused by alkaline (limy or chalky) soil or compost, lack of a sufficient water supply, or lack of fertilizer.

SIXTY OF THE BEST

Here is a guide to 60 of the best of the camellia varieties described on pages 8-13. Many will be available from garden centres, the rest from specialist nurseries.

THE COMMON CAMELLIA

'Adolphe Audusson', semi-double, an old variety with red blooms; mid-season. Makes a large bush with arching branches.

'Alba Plena', formal double, large white flowers, mid-season. Erect bushy habit of growth.

'Apollo', semi-double, with rose-red blooms, mid-season. Vigorous.

'Arejishi', paeony form, rose-red flowers, early. Handsome, toothed leaves.

'Ave Maria', miniature formal double, pink, large leaves, mid-season to late. This is fairly new.

'Adolphe Audusson'

'Apollo'

'Blaze of Glory', paeony form, large blood-red flowers, early. The bush has a rather open habit.

'Charlotte de Rothschild', single, flat white flowers, mid-season. Forms a neat rounded bush, slow grower.

'C.M. Wilson', anemone form, large light pink blooms, mid-season.

'Contessa Lavinia Maggi', formal double, an old variety, white, striped with pink and carmine, early to late. Vigorous upright habit.

'Donckelarii', semi-double, large red flowers, often with white marbling, mid-season. Slow grower, bushy habit.

'Drama Girl', loose paeony form, salmon pink, mid-season. Vigorous grower, best grown under glass if possible.

'Elegans', anemone form, an old variety with large rose-pink blooms, mid-season. Spreading habit of growth.

'Charlotte de Rothschild'

'C.M. Wilson'

'Contessa Lavinia Maggi'

'Donckelarii'

'**Guilio Nuccio**', semi-double, very large coral-pink flowers, mid-season. Vigorous, erect habit.

'**Hawaii**', paeony form, large blooms of pink and white, mid-season to late.

'**Joseph Pfingstl**', formal double or paeony form, large salmon red blooms, mid-season to late. Dense, narrow upright bush.

'**Jupiter**', single, an old variety with large crimson-red blooms, mid-season.

'**Lady Clare**', semi-double, an old variety with large salmon-pink blooms, mid-season to late. A large, rounded spreading bush.

'**Lady Vansittart**', semi-double, medium-sized flowers, white, striped with bright pink, mid-season. Bushy habit.

'**Mathotiana**', double or formal double, large crimson flowers, mid-season. Upright habit.

'**Mathotiana Alba**', formal double, large white flowers, mid-season. Vigorous habit and likes a sheltered position.

'**Matterhorn**', formal double, a new variety with white blooms, mid-season to late. Upright grower, with curving branches.

'**Miss Universe**', formal double, a fairly new variety, large white blooms, late. Spreading habit of growth.

'**Nagasaki**', semi-double, large red flowers marbled with white, mid-season. Leaves may occasionally be splashed with yellow.

'**Jupiter**'

'Joseph Pfingstl'

'Lady Clare'

'**Nobilissima**', paeony form, medium-sized flowers, white, flushed with yellow, early. Erect habit.

'**R.L. Wheeler**', anemone form, very large salmon pink flower, mid-season. Loose or open habit of growth.

'**Scentsation**', paeony form, fairly new, huge blooms, pink, mid-season, the blooms being scented (more noticeable under glass). Bushy habit of growth.

'**Taro-an**', single, pale pink, early to mid-season. Pendulous habit.

'**Tomorrow**', paeony form, large rose-red flowers, mid-season to late. A vigorous spreading bush.

'**Tricolor**', single, striped red, pink and white, mid-season. Crinkled leaves, rather holly-like.

'**Yours Truly**', semi-double, pink and white, late. Upright bush of moderate size.

'Tricolor'

'Yours Truly'

44

'Anticipation'

'Brigadoon'

'Donation'

WILLIAMSII VARIETIES

'Anticipation', full paeony form, crimson-rose blooms, early. Small, upright bush ideal for limited space, very hardy.

'Bow Bells', single, pink bell-shaped flowers, early. Compact bushy plants, very hardy, ideal for north wall.

'Bowen Bryant', semi-double, clear rose flowers, mid-season. Upright growth, very hardy.

'Brigadoon', semi-double, deep pink, mid-season. Upright habit, very hardy in all parts of Britain.

'Charles Colbert', semi-double, cream-pink blooms, mid-season. A large grower, good for hedges.

'Debbie', full paeony, rose-pink blooms, early. Vigorous grower.

'Donation', semi-double, justifiably the most popular camellia of all time, with large pink blooms, mid-season. A large bush, very hardy in all parts of Britain.

'E.G. Waterhouse', formal double, light pink, mid-season. Narrow, upright habit, ideal for limited space.

'Elegant Beauty', paeony form, rose-pink, mid-season. Excellent for training on a north wall.

'Elsie Jury', anemone or paeony form, bright pink, mid-season. Upright habit, needs plenty of sun.

'Freedom Bell', semi-double, bright red, mid-season. A small grower and very hardy in all parts of Britain.

'**Inspiration**', semi-double, deep pink, mid-season. Tall but upright, and very hardy in all parts of Britain.

'**J.C. Williams**', single, pink, early, very free flowering. Extremely hardy, ideal for training on a north wall.

'**Joan Trehane**', rose form double, rose pink, mid-season. Vigorous, tall.

'**Leonard Messel**', loose paeony, deep pink and apricot, mid-season. Very hardy.

'**Mary Larcom**', single, light pink, mid-season. Bushy, spreading habit of growth.'

'**November Pink**', single, rose-pink, early. Spreading habit of growth.

'**Rosemary Williams**', single, rose-pink, mid-season. Rather spreading habit.

'**St. Ewe**', single, rose-pink, early. Compact, upright habit and very hardy.

'**Tiptoe**', semi-double, pale pink, mid-season. Very dense growth and ideal for hedges.

'J.C. Williams'

'Inspiration'

'November Pink'

CAMELLIA RETICULATA

'**Capt. Rawes**', semi-double or paeony form, carmine-rose, late. Capable of forming a small tree in very mild areas.

'**Dream Castle**', semi-double or paeony form, pink, mid-season, very free flowering. Makes a small tree in mild areas.

'**Elsie Dryden**', semi-double, pink, very early flowering. An old but reliable variety.

'**Robert Fortune**', formal double or rose form, crimson-red, mid-season. Forms a compact bush.

'**Valentine Day**', formal double, salmon pink, early to mid-season. A slow grower out of doors but extremely free flowering.

CAMELLIA SASANQUA

'**Bert Jones**', this one has semi-double flowers in silvery pink. Growth is very strong and vigorous making it an ideal variety for wall training.

'**Narumi-gata**', single, cup-shaped flowers, white, edged with pink. An upright habit of growth.

'**Plantation Pink**', single, pink. Has a very vigorous habit of growth.

'**Tanya**', single, rose-pink flowers. Ideal for a small garden, being a low grower but with spreading growth.

'**Yuletide**', single, orange-red, with conspicuous yellow stamens. An erect habit of growth.

'Captain Rawes'

INDEX AND ACKNOWLEDGEMENTS

Anemone forms, 9, **11**

buying, 16-17

Camellia chrysantha, 7
'Cornish Snow', 10, **10**, 13
japonica, 6, 9, 13, 35, 40-4
j. 'Adolphe Audusson', 6, **27**
j. 'Ave Maria', 8
j. 'C.M. Wilson' **9**
j. 'Contessa Lavinia Maggi', **22**
j. 'Drama Girl', 8, **9**
j. 'Elegans', 9, **24**
j. 'Joseph Pfingstl', 15
j. 'Jupiter', 21
j. 'Lady Vansittart', **31**
j. 'Yours Truly', 5, 6
maliflora, 12
oleifera, 12
reticulata, 10-11, 13, **15**, 47
r. 'Captain Rawes', **27**

r. 'Dream Castle', 13
saluensis, 10, 11, **27**
sasanqua, 11, 13, 34, 47
s. 'Tricolor', **28**
sinensis, 6, 7, **7**, 12
x *williamsii*, 10, 45-6
x *w.* 'Anticipation', 8, 13, 15, **16**
x *w.* 'Bow Bells', 13
x *w.* 'Bowen Bryant', 13
x *w.* 'Brigadoon', 13, **28**
x *w.* 'Debbie', 13, **31**
x *w.* 'Donation', 8, **10**, 13, **14, 19, 22, 25**
x *w.* 'E.G. Waterhouse', 8, 15
x *w.* 'Elegant Beauty', **12**, 13
x *w.* 'Freedom Bell', 13
x *w.* 'Inspiration', 7, 13, **17, 33**
x *w.* 'J.C.

Williams', 8, 13, **25**
x *w.* 'Joan Trehane', 9, **9**
x *w.* 'Leonard Messel', 13
x *w.* 'November Pink'
x *w.* 'St Ewe', 13, **13, 27**
x *w.* 'Tiptoe', 15
choosing plants, 16
common camellia *see Camellia japonica*
companion plants, 14-15
composts, 28, 30
conservatories, 6, 32-3
containers, 26-31
cuttings, 34

diseases, 37

feeding, 21-2, 30
formal double flowers, 8, *11*

grafting, 35
greenhouses, 6, 7, 32-3

hedges, 15, **20**, 21, 25
history, 7

houseplants, 17
humidity, 18

insulation, of pots, 31

mulching, 22

north-facing walls, 13
nurseries, 17

paeony forms, 8, **11**
pests, 37
pH, 18
planting, 19-20, 29
pots, 26-8
propagation, 34-6
pruning, 24

raised beds, 19
rose forms, 9

seeds, growing from, 36
semi-double flowers, 8
shade, 18
single flowers, 8, **11**
soil, 6, 14, 18
species, 12

tea plant, 6, 7, **7**
transplanting, 20-1
tubs, 26-31

varieties, 8-11

watering, 22, 31
weed control, 23

Picture credits

Front cover: Harry Smith Horticultural Photographic Collection
Back cover: Harry Smith Horticultural Photographic Collection

A-Z Collection: 6(t,b),7,8/9,9(b),13,19,21(t),26(r),28,28/9, 32,33,40(t,b),41(br),44(r),46(tr),47
Pat Brindley: 4/5
Miki Slingsby: 38/9, 45(t)
Harry Smith Horticultural Photographic Collection: 9(t),10,12,14,15(t,b),16, 17,21(b),22/3,24,25,26(l),27(t,b),44(l),45(c,b),46(l,br)
Michael Warren: 31(b)
Colin Watmough: 23

Artwork by Richard Prideaux & Steve Sandilands